DICTATORSHIP

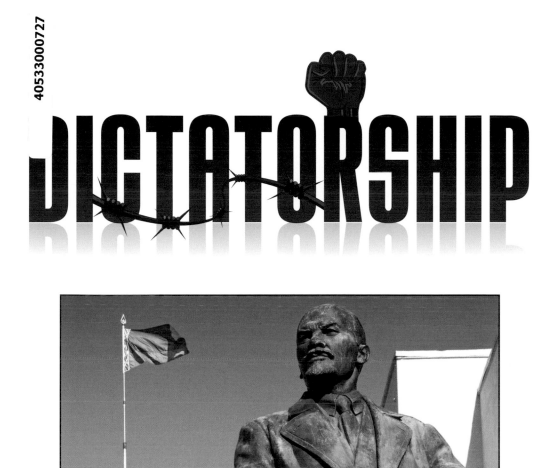

DIANE BAILEY

MASON CREST
PHILADELPHIA

Mason Crest
370 Reed Road, Suite 302
Broomall, PA 19008
www.MasonCrest.com

Printed and bound in the United States of America

CPSIA Compliance Information: Batch #MEG2012-3. For further information, contact Mason Crest at 1-866-MCP-Book.

First printing
1 3 5 7 9 8 6 4 2

Library of Congress Cataloging-in-Publication Data

Bailey, Diane, 1966-
  Dictatorship / Diane Bailey.
      p. cm. – (Major forms of world government)
  Includes bibliographical references and index.
  ISBN 978-1-4222-2138-9 (hc)
  ISBN 978-1-4222-9455-0 (ebook)
  1. Dictatorship–Juvenile literature. I. Title.
  JC495.B28 2013
  321.9–dc23
                                    2012027899

TITLES IN THIS SERIES

COMMUNISM	MILESTONES	MONARCHY
DEMOCRACY	IN THE EVOLUTION	OLIGARCHY
DICTATORSHIP	OF GOVERNMENT	THEOCRACY
FASCISM		

TABLE OF CONTENTS

INTRODUCTION by Dr. Timothy Colton, Harvard University

When human beings try to understand complex sets of things, they usually begin by sorting them into categories. They classify or group the phenomena that interest them into boxes that are basically very much alike. These boxes can then be compared and analyzed. The logic of classification applies to the study of inanimate objects (such as, for example, bodies of water or minerals), to living organisms (such as species of birds or bacteria), and also to man-made systems (such as religions or communications media).

This series of short books is about systems of government, which are specific and very important kinds of man-made systems. Systems of government are arrangements for human control and cooperation on particular territories. Governments dispense justice, make laws, raise taxes, fight wars, run school and health systems, and perform many other services that we often take for granted. Like, say, minerals, bacteria, and religions, systems of government come in a wide variety of forms or categories.

Just what are those categories? One of the earliest attempts to answer this question rigorously was made in the fourth century BCE by the brilliant Greek philosopher Aristotle. His study *Politics* has come down to us in incomplete form, as many of his writings were lost after he died. Nonetheless, it contains a simple and powerful scheme for classifying systems of government. Aristotle researched and illustrated his treatise by looking at the constitutions of 158 small city-states near the eastern shores of the Mediterranean Sea of his day, most of them inhabited by Greeks.

According to Aristotle's *Politics*, any system of government could be accurately classified and thus understood once two things were known. The first was, how many people were involved in making political decisions: one person, a small number, or a large number. The second issue was whether the system was designed to serve the common good of the citizens of the city-state. Taken together, these distinctions produced six categories of governmental system in all: monarchy (rule by one civic-minded person); tyranny (rule by one selfish person); aristocracy (rule by the few in the interests of all); oligarchy (rule by the few to suit themselves); constitutional government or "polity" (rule by the many in the common interest); and finally a form of mob rule (rule by the many with no concern for the greater good).

The fifth of these classic categories comes closest to modern representative democracy, as it is experienced in the United States, Western Europe, India, and many other places. One of the things Aristotle teaches us, however, is that there are many alternatives to this setup. In addition to the volume on democracy, this Mason Crest series will acquaint students with systems of government that correspond in rough terms to other categories invented by Aristotle more than two thousand years ago. These include monarchy; dictatorship (in Aristotle's terms, tyranny); oligarchy; communism (which we might think of as a particular kind of modern-day oligarchy); fascism (which combines some of the characteristics of tyranny and mob rule); and theocracy (which does not fit easily into Aristotle's scheme, although we might think of it as tyranny or oligarchy, but in the name of some divine being or creed).

Aristotle focused his research on the written constitutions of city-states. Today, political scientists, with better tools at their disposal, delve more into the actual practice of government in different countries. That practice frequently differs from the theory written into the constitution. Scholars study why it is that countries differ so much in terms of how and in whose interests governmental decisions are taken, across broad categories and within these categories, as well as in mixed systems that cross the boundaries between categories. It turns out that there are not one but many reasons for these differences, and there are significant disagreements about which reasons are most important. Some of the reasons are examined in this book series.

Experts on government also wonder a lot about trends over time. Why is it that some version of democracy has come to be the most common form of government in the contemporary world? Why has democratization come in distinct waves, with long periods of stagnation or even of reverse de-democratization separating them? The so-called third wave of democratization began in the 1970s and extended into the 1990s, and featured, among other changes, the collapse of communist systems in the Soviet Union and Eastern Europe and the disintegration of differently constituted nondemocratic systems in Southern Europe and Latin America. At the present time, the outlook for democracy is uncertain. In a number of Arab countries, authoritarian systems of government have recently been overthrown or challenged by revolts. And yet, it is far from clear that the result will be functioning democracies. Moreover, it is far from clear that the world will not encounter another wave of de-democratization. Nor can we rule out the rise of fundamentally new forms of government not foreseen by Aristotle; these might be encouraged by contemporary forms of technology and communication, such as the Internet, behavioral tracking devices, and social media.

For young readers to be equipped to consider complex questions like these, they need to begin with the basics about existing and historical systems of government. It is to meet their educational needs that this book series is aimed.

Robert Mugabe, president of Zimbabwe, speaks at an international conference. The dictator, in power since 1980, has been condemned by the international community for the human rights abuses and pervasive corruption of his government.

THE PURSUIT OF POWER

At one time, Robert Mugabe was hailed as a hero. A teacher by training, Mugabe became a leader in his country's struggle against colonial domination. When that struggle succeeded, and Zimbabwe won independence, voters in the southern African country elected Mugabe to serve as prime minister. His landslide victory testified to the high esteem in which he was held.

Mugabe promised to bring together all Zimbabweans. He said he would govern for the benefit of everyone. What he has actually done, over the course of three decades in power, couldn't be more different.

INDEPENDENCE LEADER

For much of the 20th century, what is now called Zimbabwe was under British control. White settlers first arrived in the region from South Africa during the late 1800s. They put down resistance by indigenous blacks and established the colony of Southern Rhodesia. Over the decades, the white minority consolidated its power. A 1930 law was particularly significant. It restricted blacks' access to land, ensuring that many blacks would be perpetually impoverished. The law sparked long-running opposition to colonial rule.

In 1964 Ian Smith became Southern Rhodesia's prime minister. He lobbied the British government to grant independence for the colony. Britain balked, because Smith insisted on preserving white-minority rule. So in 1965 Smith's government unilaterally declared independence. The new state would be known simply as Rhodesia.

The international community refused to accept Rhodesian independence. Neighboring South Africa—whose white-minority government systematically oppressed its own black citizens—was the only country to officially recognize Rhodesia. Yet neither diplomatic isolation nor international economic sanctions appeared to have much effect on Smith's government.

For his part, Robert Mugabe was an eloquent and outspoken critic of white-minority rule. Born in 1924, Mugabe became the secretary general of a black nationalist party, the Zimbabwe African National Union (ZANU), in the early 1960s. In 1964 the Rhodesian government banned ZANU and arrested its leaders.

Mugabe spent a decade as a political prisoner. He was released in late 1974. Within a year, he had become the undisputed head of ZANU. From exile in Mozambique, he helped direct a guerrilla war against the Rhodesian government.

By the late 1970s, military pressure from the Patriotic Front—an opposition alliance that included ZANU and another nationalist party, the Zimbabwe African People's Union (ZAPU)—had finally convinced Smith's government to negotiate an end to white-minority rule. At a British-sponsored peace conference held in 1979, representatives of the Rhodesian government and the Patriotic Front agreed to a new constitution and democratic elections open to blacks as well as whites.

By 1978, more than 40,000 residents of Southern Rhodesia had become refugees, fleeing the civil war in the country. This photo shows a refugee camp in Mozambique. The heavy toll taken by the war led to a cease-fire agreement in 1979 and independence for the country, now called Zimbabwe, in April 1980. In the first national election, Robert Mugabe's ZANU party won control of the new country's government.

Those elections, held in February 1980, resulted in a landslide victory for the ZANU party. Robert Mugabe thus became the first prime minister of the newly independent country of Zimbabwe.

Many white Zimbabweans worried that the black majority would seek retribution after decades of oppression. The new prime minister sought to allay these fears. He promised that the rights of all citizens would be respected. "If yesterday I fought you as an enemy," Mugabe said on the day of his inauguration, "today you have become a friend and ally with the same national interests, loyalty, rights and duties as myself. . . . Our majority rule could easily turn into inhuman rule if we oppressed, persecuted or harassed those of us who do not look or think like the majority of us."

DESTROYING THE JEWEL OF AFRICA

Two other African heads of state sent Zimbabwe's new leader words of encouragement. "You have the jewel of Africa in your hands," President Julius Nyerere of Tanzania and President Samora Machel of Mozambique noted. "Now look after it."

On a continent beset by problems, Zimbabwe was indeed conspicuous for its gleaming advantages. It had good infrastructure, including fine railways and roads. Its soil and climate conditions were ideal for the cultivation of a wide variety of crops, and Zimbabwe boasted one of Africa's most productive agricultural sectors. It also had significant mineral resources, including gold, platinum, and coal. In short, there seemed little reason why the country couldn't flourish. All it needed was good governance.

Unfortunately, Robert Mugabe did not deliver good governance. In fact, he became one of the world's most notorious, corrupt, and brutal dictators. In the process, he devastated Zimbabwe.

Mugabe's evolution from hero of independence to cruel tyrant began soon after his election as prime minister. In 1981 Mugabe announced his intention to transform Zimbabwe into a socialist state—and he openly called for violence against anyone who opposed

To consolidate his own power, Mugabe dismissed fellow independence leader Joshua Nkomo (pictured here) from his government in 1982. In the civil war that resulted, Mugabe unleashed his private military force, the Fifth Brigade, to attack and terrorize civilians who supported Nkomo.

his plans. Mugabe built an elite military force known as the Fifth Brigade. It was never integrated into Zimbabwe's regular army. Instead, it was answerable only to the prime minister. The Fifth Brigade became Mugabe's personal army.

In 1982 Mugabe dismissed one of his ministers, Joshua Nkomo. The move would have serious repercussions. Nkomo was the leader of the ZAPU party, whose rivalry with Mugabe's ZANU was based largely on ethnicity. ZAPU drew its support from the Ndebele minority, which was concentrated in southern and western Zimbabwe. ZANU, by contrast, represented the majority Shona, Mugabe's ethnic group. After Nkomo's dismissal, a civil war erupted.

> ## KEY IDEA
>
> Dictators often maintain the trappings of democracy, such as elections and a representative legislature. But they hold actual power.

The Fifth Brigade was deployed to help put down Ndebele rebels. It earned a reputation for targeting civilians. Fifth Brigade soldiers would enter villages, command residents to voice their support for Mugabe, and then torture several people in front of their families. Mugabe's troops also routinely blocked the delivery of food supplies, causing civilians to starve to death.

Zimbabwe's civil war was finally brought to an end in 1987, when Mugabe and Nkomo agreed to merge their respective parties into the Zimbabwe African National Union–Patriotic Front (ZANU-PF). That same year, Mugabe spearheaded a change to the country's constitution. The position of prime minister was abolished in favor of a president, with Mugabe serving in that office. This and other changes to the constitution concentrated more power in Mugabe's hands.

Meanwhile, government jobs increasingly went to Mugabe's supporters. Many used their positions as a means to enrich themselves at the public's expense. They doled out jobs to friends and relatives. Educated, qualified Zimbabweans were unable to find professional employment simply because they didn't have connections. The country's economy faltered under the weight of corruption and mismanagement. Government services were abysmal. Zimbabwe's infrastructure, once the envy of Africa, fell into disrepair.

LAND GRAB

Conditions grew infinitely worse after 2000, when Mugabe initiated the "fast-track land resettlement program." He portrayed it as a means of achieving much-needed land reform. Critics charged that the program was conceived mostly as a way to strengthen Mugabe's grip on power.

There was certainly a strong case for land reform in Zimbabwe. Decades of white rule had left most of the country's black people landless. The 1979 agreement that led to Zimbabwe's independence promised to correct this historical injustice. Large white-owned farms would be purchased, and the land redistributed to blacks to cultivate. But the white farmers were supposed to be offered a fair price for their land, and they weren't supposed to be coerced into selling. However, under the fast-track land resettlement program, armed ZANU-PF members—often with support from police—invaded white-owned commercial farms. Using threats or actual violence, they expelled the white farmers and, in many cases, the black agricultural laborers who worked for those farmers.

Large parcels of seized land were claimed by Mugabe's inner circle. The president, too, would create his own huge estate from 10,000 acres of prime land taken from white farmers.

For ordinary Zimbabweans, the path to owning a farm was less certain. Those who applied for land grants first had to demonstrate support for ZANU-PF and Robert Mugabe. Anyone suspected of disloyalty was rejected.

The rapid breakup of white-owned commercial farms had severe consequences for Zimbabwe. Many of the new black farmers lacked the knowledge, experience, and money needed to run a large-scale enterprise. Agricultural production plummeted. Zimbabwe, once an exporter of food,

Under Mugabe, the government of Zimbabwe declared many large farms and desirable tracts of land to be "state property." The government turned ownership over to Mugabe's friends or supporters without compensating the previous owners.

could no longer feed its own people. Inflation soared. The entire economy spiraled downward, and millions of Zimbabweans were plunged into abject poverty.

Mugabe showed little concern for the plight of Zimbabwe's people. Nor did he tolerate opposition. If judicial decisions displeased him, he simply overturned those decisions. In 2002 he responded to mounting criticism by cracking down on freedom of the press. That same year, he claimed another term as president in elections international observers deemed seriously flawed.

By the time the next presidential elections were held, in 2008, Mugabe appeared to be in danger of losing his grip on power. Zimbabwe's citizens were desperate for change. After nearly three decades of rule by Mugabe, their country was a basket case. Unemployment topped 80 percent. Runaway inflation made the country's currency essentially worthless. Eight in every 10 schools had been shuttered. An estimated 50 percent of Zimbabweans were hungry or in danger of starvation. The majority of hospitals had been closed because of a lack of medicines and other supplies. Water in the cities was no longer safe to drink, and cholera had broken out in several places.

In March 2008 presidential voting, Morgan Tsvangirai of the Movement for Democratic Change (MDC) outpolled Mugabe and another opposition candidate in a three-way race. However, Mugabe claimed—falsely, many

Morgan Tsvangirai (left), leader of Zimbabwe's Movement for Democratic Change (MDC), meets with United Nations Secretary-General Ban Ki-moon in Ghana, 2008. That year, Tsvangirai outpolled Mugabe and another candidate in a three-way race for the presidency. However, according to the official count, Tsvangirai failed to gain the absolute majority required by Zimbabwe's constitution. A runoff election was scheduled for June, but Tsvangirai withdrew in the face of a vicious campaign of violence targeting his supporters. That left Mugabe as the only candidate in the election, and he won a new presidential term easily with 86 percent of the vote.

Once considered a hero by Africans for leading Zimbabwe to independence, Robert Mugabe today is considered one of the world's most abusive dictators.

independent observers suspected—that Tsvangirai had failed to win an absolute majority of the vote. Under Zimbabwe's constitution, this meant that a runoff election was necessary.

In advance of the June runoff, government forces unleashed a brutal campaign, called "Operation Let Us Finish Them Off." It targeted MDC members and voters thought to have cast their ballots for Tsvangirai. Tens of thousands were set upon by machete- and ax-wielding agents of the government. "They killed hundreds of people, but they tortured vast numbers of people," journalist Peter Godwin reported. "And then they released them back to their communities so they acted like human billboards—they were advertisements for what happens if you oppose the regime."

In the runoff election, Mugabe claimed fully twice as many votes as the official count had given him credit for just four months earlier. International observers decried the election as a sham. Regardless, Mugabe retained the presidency.

And, as of the summer of 2012, Mugabe was still in power. He continued to terrorize political opponents. He and his cronies continued to loot Zimbabwe. The 88-year-old dictator vowed to live to be 100.

A gold-plated statue of Saparmurat Niyazov, the first president of Turkmenistan, stands atop this enormous monument in Ashgabat, the country's capital. While ruling Turkmenistan with absolute power from 1991 to 2006, the dictator created a "cult of personality" in which he was portrayed as an infallible leader who always acted in the best interests of the entire nation.

2

THE DICTATOR'S RULE

"**P**ower tends to corrupt," observed the 19th-century English historian Lord Acton, "and absolute power corrupts absolutely." The case of Robert Mugabe is a good illustration of Acton's famous dictum. By all accounts, Mugabe was concerned with the welfare of his nation when he first took office as Zimbabwe's prime minister. Over time, however, his actions began to reveal an entirely different agenda. Mugabe accrued more and more authority, which he used in the service of a personal goal: to ensure that he remained in power. He became completely unaccountable. He didn't respect the will of voters. He didn't respect the legal system. While Mugabe and a circle of close supporters helped themselves to Zimbabwe's wealth, the rest of the country suffered. Anyone who challenged the situation was dealt with harshly.

Mugabe's story is hardly unique. Other leaders have won democratic elections, only to assume dictatorial powers once in office. François "Papa Doc" Duvalier had exiled most of his political opponents within a month of his October 1957 election as Haiti's president. By the end of the year, Duvalier had pushed through a new constitution giving him more authority. He would rule Haiti with an iron fist until his death in 1971.

Ugandans elected Yoweri Museveni president in 1996 and reelected him in 2001. For a while, Museveni earned praise—in Uganda and abroad—for his apparent dedication to democracy and good governance. But then he had Uganda's constitution amended to do away with presidential term limits. The change enabled him to run for a third term, and in 2006 he claimed victory in an election tarnished by the arrest of his main opponent on treason charges, censorship of the press, voter intimidation,

During the 1970s, Yoweri Museveni helped lead a rebellion against Uganda's corrupt dictator, Idi Amin. Elected president in 1996 and reelected in 2001, he seemed genuinely dedicated to the principles of democracy—until he forced a change in Uganda's constitution that did away with presidential term limits and allowed him to remain in power indefinitely.

and credible evidence of fraud. Museveni secured a fourth presidential term after 2011 elections that international observers deemed seriously compromised.

If the road to dictatorship is sometimes paved with ballots, more often it is paved with bullets. The list of dictators who came to power after a revolution or coup is extensive and includes representatives from every inhabited continent. A small sampling of the more famous: Benito Mussolini (Italy), Mao Zedong (China), Fidel Castro (Cuba), Idi Amin (Uganda), Muammar Gaddafi (Libya), Augusto Pinochet (Chile). In many cases dictators who take power through violent means promise to

Muammar Gaddafi used funds from the sale of Libya's oil to improve the standard of living for people in his country. Yet during his more than 40 years in power, the dictator was infamous for brutally repressing all domestic opposition, as well as for sponsoring international terrorist groups. Gaddafi was finally ousted and killed in 2011.

bring tangible benefits to their countries, such as political stability, an improved economy, or greater social justice. On occasion they deliver on some of their promises, at least for a while. Typically, however, the social, economic, and moral costs of dictatorship turn out to be quite high.

DEFINING DICTATORSHIP

The term *dictatorship* refers to a government in which arbitrary and absolute power is wielded by one person or by a small clique (such as a group of generals). Dictatorships are, by definition, undemocratic. Dictators don't govern according to limits set by a constitution. They don't respect the rule of law; rather, they are above the law. Dictators don't govern with the consent of citizens. They govern as they see fit.

All dictatorships are authoritarian regimes—they enforce obedience to the ruler's wishes—but not all authoritarian regimes qualify as dictatorships. Before the modern era, kings and queens commonly held absolute power. However, societies recognized absolute monarchy as a legitimate form of government. In many places, the authority of kings and queens was believed to be divinely bestowed. Moreover, there were established and accepted rules for the transfer of

Cuban dictator Fidel Castro speaks at the United Nations. Castro came to power by leading a revolution that overthrew another dictator, Fulgencio Batista, in 1959. However, during his six decades as ruler of Cuba, Castro used the same ruthless tactics that Batista had used in order to maintain complete control over the island nation.

power (usually the oldest male child inherited the throne upon the death of a monarch). For these reasons, absolute monarchies aren't usually classified as dictatorships. Dictators subvert the established political order. They take or hold power in a manner that is not approved by the society at large.

> ## KEY IDEA
>
> Dictators wield power not within the framework of law but rather at their own discretion.

Certain forms of government are rooted in an ideology, or systematic set of principles and goals. Communism, for example, promises economic justice through the common ownership of productive resources and the elimination of social classes. Liberal democracy is founded on the principle of majority rule and the idea that every individual has certain fundamental rights, which the government is obligated to protect.

No such guiding principles underpin dictatorship. Dictatorship is a way of holding and exercising power rather than an ideology for governance. So dictators may come from either end of the political spectrum.

LEFT, RIGHT, OR NEITHER

In the details of how they function and the specific rules they impose on citizens, dictatorships vary considerably. That shouldn't be too surprising. In addition to country-specific factors such as culture and national history, a dictatorial regime can be heavily influenced by the personal eccentricities of the dictator.

In the 20th century, political scientists developed several schemes for classifying dictatorships. One highly influential approach (which will be discussed more fully in the next chapter) divides dictatorships into two categories: authoritarian and totalitarian. Basically, the distinction between the two boils down to how much control the regime exerts.

Another widely used classification method considers the ideological orientation of the dictatorship. This approach distinguishes between right-wing and left-wing dictatorships.

Right-wing dictators use their power to uphold a conservative status quo. They vehemently oppose communism. Right-wing dictators typically make appeals to tradition, the need for order, and, in many cases, nationalism. Often they justify their seizure of power as necessary to protect society from the threat of communists. A few examples of right-wing dictators are Portugal's António de Oliveira Salazar, in power from 1932 to 1968; Spain's Francisco Franco (1939–75); and South Korea's Syngman Rhee (1948–60). The military juntas (councils) that ruled various Latin American countries from the 1950s into the 1980s are also considered right-wing dictatorships.

Since his 1999 election as president of Venezuela, Hugo Chávez has steadily increased the power of his office while arresting his political opponents. In 2010, allies in the National Assembly gave Chávez the authority to rule without input from elected legislators. Chávez's move toward dictatorship has resulted in international criticism of his regime.

Left-wing dictatorships are communist or socialist in orientation. These dictatorships seek to effect fundamental change, and they justify their power in the name of creating a more equitable society. Left-wing dictators include the Soviet Union's Vladimir Lenin, North Korea's Kim Il-sung, and China's Mao Zedong. All three ruled from the establishment of a communist state in their country until they died (Lenin in 1924, Mao in 1976, and Kim in 1994). More recently, Venezuela's Hugo Chávez, a socialist, has assumed increasingly dictatorial powers since winning a 1999 presidential election.

The right-wing/left-wing approach to classifying dictatorships may be useful, but it does have limitations. Some dictatorships don't fit easily into either category. They don't display any clear ideological orientation. Some dictators simply seem to like power. Some may be fulfilling a psychological need for self-aggrandizement. Saparmurat Niyazov, the dictator of Turkmenistan from 1990 to 2006, built thousands of monuments to himself (including golden statues); renamed a city in his honor; and even had months of the year renamed for his family members. Other dictators use their power primarily for personal enrichment. For example, Teodoro Obiang Nguema Mbasogo, who has ruled Equatorial Guinea since 1979, is believed to have plundered at least $700 million from his country's treasury. Other examples of predatory dictators abound.

ANCIENT ROME

Today, the connotations of the word *dictatorship* are almost entirely negative. That wasn't always the case. In the Roman Republic, which lasted from the sixth century BCE to the first century BCE, dictatorship was seen as a necessary recourse during certain crises.

Rome's government was normally headed by two chief civil and military magistrates, called consuls. The consuls had the power to overrule the decisions of lower magistrates. But either consul could also veto a decision made by the other. This was to protect against the accumulation of too much power in one person's hands.

However, during an emergency such as a rebellion, the Roman Senate could call for the appointment of a dictator. The dictator's powers were absolute. He was the supreme military commander and the chief executive officer of the Roman Republic. His decisions couldn't be challenged. All officeholders had to obey his orders or they would be removed—or even put to death.

The institution of dictatorship would seem to invite the destruction of Rome's republican institutions. But there were safeguards to prevent a dictator from becoming a tyrant. To begin, the Senate appointed a dictator to deal with a specific crisis, and his term could last no longer than six months. Senators themselves weren't allowed to serve as dictator. And, though his powers were vast, a dictator wasn't permitted to do away with other state institutions. The purpose of the dictatorship was to stabilize the existing governmental system, not to create a new one.

For a long time, dictatorship in the Roman Republic functioned as intended. Dictators commonly relinquished power as soon as the crisis they'd been appointed to deal with had been resolved, even if that was before their six-month term was up. Most dictators were looked on favorably, as they took power to fight off the Roman Republic's foreign enemies or to end civil wars.

The institution of the dictatorship changed dramatically in 82 BCE. That year the Roman general Sulla won a civil war with the rival general Marius and had himself named dictator. In a break with precedent, Sulla's term as dictator was open-ended rather than limited to six months. In addition, his charge wasn't to put down a rebellion or battle foreign enemies but to make laws and revise the Roman constitution. Despite the possibility for abuse, Sulla voluntarily retired after about a year as dictator.

The dictatorship wasn't invoked again until 49 BCE, when the general Julius Caesar sparked a civil war by taking his army from the Roman province of Gaul and marching on Rome. Caesar had himself appointed dictator. He served three straight one-year terms before securing appointment for a 10-year term as dictator in 46 BCE. Just two years later, however, Caesar dispensed with the charade that he ever intended to give up power, declaring himself "Dictator for Life." But members of the Senate, who were evidently concerned about Caesar's accretion of power, assassinated him in 44 BCE.

Less than 20 years later, the Roman Republic would come to an end. It was replaced by the Roman Empire. Now absolute power was concentrated in the hands of one person—the emperor—not simply during emergencies but all the time.

DICTATORSHIP IN THE MODERN ERA

Across much of the globe, monarchical forms of government predominated until recent centuries. Many kings and emperors claimed absolute power. Many ruled ruthlessly. But, as noted previously, hereditary monarchies aren't considered dictatorships.

Some historians regard Napoleon Bonaparte as the first modern dictator. In 1799, after the French Revolution had replaced the monarchy in France with

Julius Caesar wished to do away with the government of the Roman Republic, which had become corrupt and weak. After winning a civil war to become the ruler of Rome, he took power away from the city-state's democratically elected Senate in order to carry out his political reform program.

Napoleon Bonaparte (1769–1821) is sometimes called the first modern dictator.

a republican form of government, Napoleon seized power in a coup. Five years later he crowned himself emperor. Napoleon ruled until a coalition of European countries defeated him militarily in 1814.

Numerous other dictatorships emerged during in the 1800s, after a wave of revolutions swept away European colonial rule in Central and South America (and, to a lesser extent, the Caribbean). In seeking their independence, the peoples of Latin America had been inspired largely by the ideals of the American Revolution. But as they sought to create democratic institutions, the newly independent Latin American nations confronted social and political disorder. Borders were disputed. Civil wars erupted with some frequency. This turbulent environment provided favorable conditions for men to take power for themselves through military force.

The *caudillo*—Spanish for "chief" or "leader"—frequently contended with elected officials for governing authority in the decades after Latin American nations gained their independence. Caudillos had their roots in the colonial period. At most times, Spain kept a relatively small professional army in its Latin American colonies. Colonial governors relied on large civilian militias to maintain order, particularly outside of capital cities. Militia leaders usually came from the ranks of large landowners. In return for their service, they received a small salary and other perks from the Spanish crown.

Militias played a major role in winning independence from Spain, and many militia commanders emerged from the fighting as widely admired figures. Where the new national governments were unable to establish order, these commanders—caudillos—often stepped into the breach.

Using their personal prestige, their ability to provide employment for local men, and their private armies, they became unofficial regional chieftains.

Inevitably, many caudillos were tempted to intervene in national politics. Some, like Venezuela's José Antonio Páez, were relatively high-minded statesmen. Páez ruled as dictator (technically he held the office of president) on three separate occasions between the 1830s and the 1860s. But his overriding concern, in the view of many historians, was providing stability to the national government when it appeared to be teetering.

Other caudillos, by contrast, were clearly power-hungry opportunists. Mexico's Antonio López de Santa Anna is a prime example. Santa Anna took, lost, and retook power more than 10 times between the 1830s and the 1850s. His personal corruption and military misadventures proved disastrous for Mexico.

Most historians agree that the phenomenon of caudillo rule left a harmful legacy for Latin American nations. Even when, like José Antonio Páez, caudillos may have had decent motives, their methods were outside the law. Caudillos ruled through personalized power, not power conferred by a constitution. Caudillos also helped ingrain a troublesome pattern in Latin American political culture: that of seeking a military solution to the problem of social turmoil. In the process, caudillos helped pave the way for future Latin American dictatorships, including the military juntas that held power during much of the 20th century.

One of the most infamous of the Latin American caudillos was the general Antonio López de Santa Anna, who served as ruler of Mexico during 11 different periods between 1833 and 1855.

In the 20th century, the ambitions of totalitarian dictators like Benito Mussolini of Italy and Adolf Hitler of Germany plunged the world into the devastating conflict known as the Second World War.

3

AUTHORITARIANISM AND TOTALITARIANISM

Most dictators—from the caudillos and military juntas of Latin America to current-day autocrats like Robert Mugabe or Aleksandr Lukashenko of Belarus—do not seek to exercise complete control over their societies. That isn't to deny that these dictators often claim an absolute right to govern. It isn't to say that they tolerate direct opposition, or that they aren't ruthless in suppressing dissent. However, they do leave intact certain social and economic institutions. They do allow citizens a certain degree of latitude in their private lives.

In the mid-20th century, political scientists distinguished this style of limited dictatorship, called authoritarian dictatorship, from an all-encompassing form. The all-encompassing form was labeled totalitarian dictatorship. Totalitarian dictatorships seek control over all aspects of society—including economics, popular culture, even what citizens think. Totalitarianism requires the complete submission of the individual to the state.

In their influential 1956 book, *Totalitarian Dictatorship and Autocracy*, political scientists Carl J. Friedrich and Zbigniew Brzezinski identified six essential characteristics of a totalitarian dictatorship:

1. It is controlled by a single political party.
2. The ruling party controls the military.
3. The ruling party controls mass communications.
4. It has a centrally directed economy.
5. It has a secret police.
6. It has an official ideology centering on the creation of an ideal society.

Thousands of people hold a candlelight vigil in Hong Kong to remember Chinese citizens killed when the government crushed pro-democracy protests in Tiananmen Square in June 1989. Although China's government has permitted a greater degree of economic freedom since Mao Zedong's death, the state continues to repress any perceived threat to its authority.

Totalitarian dictatorships first emerged during the 1930s, in the Soviet Union and Nazi Germany. The ideologies of these two states were quite dissimilar. The former was grounded in communism; the latter, in the violently nationalistic ideology of fascism.

ROOTS OF FASCISM

Though it reached its most malignant form in Germany, fascism didn't originate there. It began in Italy.

World War I (1914–18) took a terrible toll on Europe. Italy was no exception. Some 1.5 million Italian soldiers were killed or wounded in the conflict. Many Italians blamed their government for involving the country in the war, and for the often-incompetent manner in which Italy's armed forces were commanded.

In the years immediately following the war, Italy experienced considerable turmoil. The economy was in shambles. Unemployment was high, and many veterans were unable to find jobs when they returned to civilian life. Riots and worker strikes occurred frequently.

Italy's government seemed ill equipped to deal with the problems. Italy had a democratic system—specifically, a constitutional monarchy with an elected parliament—but it was of recent origin, having been established in 1870. Italy's political parties demonstrated only a weak commitment to democracy. They bickered constantly and generally rejected compromise in favor of all-or-nothing tactics.

A former journalist and army veteran named Benito Mussolini capitalized on Italy's troubled political environment to engineer his own rise to power. In 1919 Mussolini organized followers—including many war veterans—into armed paramilitary units known as the Blackshirts. After he'd run for parliament and lost, Mussolini unleashed the Blackshirts to attack and intimidate his opponents. In 1921, when he ran for parliament again, he won.

Mussolini founded the Fascist Party. It promised to protect Italy from the threat of communism. It also called for a foreign policy of aggressive expansion.

In 1922, after Mussolini threatened a coup, he was named prime minister of Italy. Over the next few years, he consolidated his power. All political parties besides the Fascist Party were outlawed. All newspapers except those willing to print the Fascist line were closed. Blackshirts visited violence on anyone who dared speak out against Mussolini or the Fascist Party.

Mussolini used the term *totalitario* ("totalitarian") to refer to the kind of state he sought to create. Simply put, the state would exercise complete control over all aspects of life, public as well as private. Every Italian would be expected to unquestioningly serve the needs of the state—as defined by Mussolini and the Fascist Party. "The Fascist conception of life," Mussolini wrote, "stresses the importance of the State and accepts the individual only in so far as his interests coincide with those of the State."

Mussolini took the title *Il Duce* ("the Leader"). He was a compelling public speaker and possessed great charisma. But these natural gifts alone weren't enough to create the idealized public image—the cult of personality—that Mussolini sought. His regime used its control of the mass media, propaganda, and the indoctrination of young people, among other methods, to elevate Mussolini to the status of national savior. The dictator's speeches were broadcast in schools, theaters, and

The Italian dictator Benito Mussolini addresses a crowd at a rally. In the 1920s Mussolini leveraged his charisma and skill at public speaking—along with the threat of violence by his supporters—to take control of Italy's government.

public squares. When Mussolini was filmed, the cameras were positioned below him, looking up, so that he would appear taller and more heroic. The lights in his office were left on even when he was not there, to give the impression that he was working tirelessly. All public activities, such as sporting events and concerts, became occasions for extolling Mussolini and celebrating the Fascist Party.

What Fascism promised Italians was a return to national glory. More specifically, Mussolini pledged to create a new empire that would rival in power and splendor the empire of ancient Rome. This vision became a sort of political religion, and Mussolini was venerated (or at least sought to be venerated) as a godlike figure who would make it a reality. "I believe in the genius of Mussolini," Italian children recited at the beginning of each school day, "in our Holy Father Fascism, in the communion of its martyrs, in the conversion of Italians and in the resurrection of the Empire."

For several reasons, including compromises with the Catholic Church and Italy's popular monarchy, Mussolini never succeeded in establishing a totalitarian state. But he inspired another dictator who did: Adolf Hitler.

HITLER AND THE NAZIS

Hitler was a disillusioned veteran of World War I when, in late 1919, he joined a small and marginal German political party. It would become the Nazi Party, and by 1921 Hitler was its leader.

Germany, even more than Italy, was in a state of disarray after World War I. It had been defeated in the war, at a cost of at least 1.7 million dead. Its economy was ruined. The German monarchy had been swept away, but the democratic government that replaced it—known as the Weimar Republic—was weak. There were assassinations and riots. Rival political factions even fought pitched battles in the streets of German cities.

Using Mussolini's Blackshirts as a model, Hitler established the Brownshirts—officially, the Sturmabteilung (German for "Storm Troopers"). The Nazi paramilitary organization quickly developed a reputation for brutally attacking opponents. In 1923 Hitler, with support from Brownshirt units, tried to overthrow the Weimar government. The coup attempt failed miserably, however. Hitler and a handful of other Nazis received brief prison sentences as a result.

After emerging from prison in late 1924, Hitler settled on a new strategy for gaining power. The Nazi Party would temporarily work within the democratic system, campaigning for seats in the Reichstag, Germany's parliament. At the same time, the Nazis would build a mass movement. They would attract large numbers of ordinary people to the party and its message.

The Nazis didn't offer many specific policies. Instead, they emphasized broad themes that evoked powerful emotions like fear, hatred, and pride. One recurring theme was the threat of communism. Another was anti-Semitism. The Nazis blamed Jews for many of Germany's problems. They claimed that Jews had helped betray the country during World War I. They also said that Jews were racially inferior and had polluted the blood of "true" Germans, who the Nazis said had descended from a "master race" called the Aryans. Another major theme was the promise to restore German greatness—a promise that implied both restrictions on Germany's Jews and aggression against other nations.

In the years 1925–1929, membership in the Nazi Party grew steadily, from about 27,000 to more than 100,000. Still, the Nazis failed to make inroads in the Reichstag. Germany's economy had improved, and the political system seemed relatively stable. In this environment, voters weren't attracted to the Nazis' extreme message.

By the early 1930s, however, that had changed. The worldwide economic crisis known as the Great Depression was wreaking havoc in Germany. Unemployment had spiked. Many Germans were plunged into desperate poverty. Crime rose. German society seemed to be on the verge of breaking apart. Adolf Hitler promised strong leadership to deal with the country's problems, and German voters responded. The Nazi Party became the largest in the Reichstag, though it never gained a majority of seats.

In January 1933 Hitler was appointed chancellor, Germany's head of state. A month later, Nazis secretly set a fire in the Reichstag building.

Hitler used the fire—which the Nazis blamed on a communist conspiracy—as a pretext for obtaining an emergency decree. It allowed him to suspend Germans' civil rights.

From that point on, Hitler moved quickly to consolidate his power. In March 1933 an act passed by the Reichstag gave him dictatorial authority. That same month the first of many Nazi concentration camps, Dachau, was set up. Actual or suspected opponents of the regime were sent to the camp, where they endured brutal treatment. Prisoners were never told when they would be released, if ever. By July 1933 all political parties other than the Nazi Party had been outlawed.

Restrictions targeting Jewish people began almost as soon as the Nazis came to power and became more and more severe as the years passed. Eventually, Germany's Jews—along with Jews living in countries that Germany conquered during World War II—would be sent to concentration camps or death camps. In the former, they performed slave labor until they died of disease, exhaustion, or starvation. In the latter, they were murdered, usually with poison gas. All told, the Holocaust—Nazi Germany's systematic effort to exterminate Europe's entire Jewish population—would claim an estimated 6 million lives.

During the 1920s and 1930s, Adolf Hitler attracted followers by promising to create a glorious new Germany. This appealed to many Germans who were unhappy with the way their country had been punished by the Allied Powers after World War I.

But Jews weren't the only group the Nazis targeted for elimination. In the name of racial "hygiene" (health), about 200,000 Germans who had a physical disability, a mental illness, or Down syndrome were also methodically killed.

The full scope of the Nazis' atrocities emerged only in 1945, after Germany's defeat in World War II. Across the globe, people saw gruesome photos from concentration camps and wondered: How could the German people have permitted this to happen? Why had millions of ordinary Germans done nothing as their government carried out its campaign of genocide? Why had many other Germans willingly participated in the atrocities?

There are no easy answers to these questions. But at least part of the explanation lies in the nature of the Nazi totalitarian state.

From the time the Nazis took power, the German people were subjected to a never-ending barrage of propaganda. Much of it centered on the person of Adolf Hitler. The Führer ("leader") was portrayed in superhuman terms. He was infallible. He alone could lead Germany to a glorious future. The German people had only obey. "With pride we see that one man remains beyond all criticism, that is the Führer," noted Rudolf Hess, Hitler's deputy. "This is because everyone feels and knows: he is always right, and he will always be right."

The establishment of youth organizations ensured that, away from the influence of their parents, young Germans would be indoctrinated in Nazi ideas and the cult of the Führer. Between the ages of 10 and 18, all ethnically German, non-Jewish youngsters had to belong to a Nazi youth organization. Males were enrolled in the Hitler Youth; females, in the League of German Girls. The youngsters were drilled constantly on the importance of maintaining Aryan racial purity, and on the evil of Jews. They also swore an oath of loyalty to Hitler.

If their propaganda and indoctrination efforts were designed to instill loyalty to Hitler, the Nazis also used coercion and fear to keep Germans in line. Citizens who spoke out against the regime were subject to arrest, imprisonment, and even death. They had no legal protections. Even the mere suspicion that someone opposed the regime could land that person in trouble. The Nazis' secret police organization, called the Gestapo, maintained an extensive network of citizen informers. People could never know when someone might report them to the authorities. Germans lived in constant terror. According to the political philosopher Hannah Arendt, this terror is at the heart of totalitarianism.

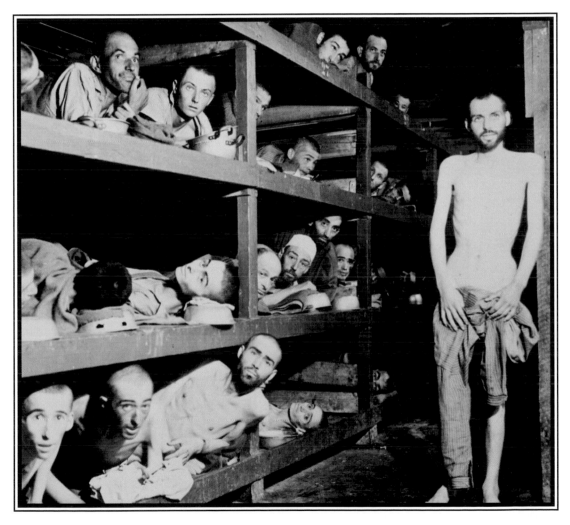

Jewish slave laborers in a barracks at the Buchenwald concentration camp near Jena, Germany. The Nazi regime demonized and, ultimately, sought to exterminate Jews.

THE SOVIET UNION UNDER STALIN

Joseph Stalin was certainly well versed in the uses of terror. Stalin, who ruled the Soviet Union for a quarter century, used terror both to advance communist policies and to keep himself in power. He also created a cult of personality that was every bit as unrestrained as that of Hitler, taking titles such as "Brilliant Genius of Humanity," "Gardener of Human Happiness," and "Father of Nations."

After the death of the Soviet Union's founder, Vladimir Lenin, in 1924, various Communist Party leaders maneuvered to succeed him. With a few years, Stalin had won this power struggle. He proceeded to transform the Soviet Union from an authoritarian to a totalitarian state.

Communism seeks the elimination of private property. Stalin pursued that goal wholeheartedly. In 1928 he started bringing the entire Soviet economy under the control of the state. One crucial step involved moving peasants from their own small plots of land onto large, state-run collective farms. Many peasants resisted collectivization, however. They had no desire to work on collectives but instead wanted to continue farming their own land. Stalin responded brutally. Some peasants were executed. Others were sent to the gulag, a network of slave-labor camps that were located mostly in remote Siberia.

Stalin dealt with the peasants of one region, the Ukraine, even more harshly. He ordered soldiers to seize huge amounts of grain there. As a result, an estimated 5 million Ukrainians died of starvation in 1932 and 1933.

Between 1925 and 1953, while Joseph Stalin was in power in the Soviet Union, policies such as forced collectivization and ruthless political purges resulted in an estimated 20 million deaths.

In 1936 Stalin launched a political campaign that would become known as the Great Purge. It was designed to eliminate anyone who might threaten his rule. The NKVD, the Soviet Union's secret police, arrested prominent Communist Party officials and military leaders. With little or no supporting evidence, these people were accused of plotting against the government. They were tortured, and many not only confessed to the most outlandish plots but also implicated other supposed traitors. Many of the accused were executed. Many others were sent to the gulag.

The Great Purge continued even after Stalin's potential rivals in the Communist Party and the military had been eliminated. Ordinary citizens were picked up and questioned by the NKVD. When threatened or tortured, some accused co-workers, neighbors, friends—in certain cases, even family members—of disloyalty to the Soviet Union. It was impossible to know whether, or when, some baseless accusation might lead to one's arrest and execution. This unpredictability created a profound sense of terror.

By the time the Great Purge finally ended in 1938, millions of Soviet citizens had been arrested and imprisoned. Historians believe that anywhere from about 700,000 to 1.2 million people were killed in the purge.

Stalin's brutal methods proved effective. He remained in power until his death in 1953.

MAO ZEDONG

Like Joseph Stalin, China's Mao Zedong created a totalitarian dictatorship in the name of a communist ideology. Mao, like his Soviet counterpart, pursued a program of rural collectivization and launched ruthless campaigns to eliminate political opposition. He nurtured a cult of personality as the "Great Helmsman," a bold and brilliant leader charting a path of progress for his country. But in China, as in the Soviet Union, the human toll of totalitarian dictatorship was appalling.

The People's Republic of China was officially proclaimed on October 1, 1949, after communist forces led by Mao emerged victorious in a civil war. Soon Mao's government set about restructuring China's economy. In the cities, privately owned businesses and industries were brought under the control of the state. In the vast countryside, a campaign of land reform was undertaken. Its ultimate goal was to abolish private ownership of land and organize China's half-billion rural residents on large collectives.

Many Chinese intellectuals were unhappy about the policies of the government. Many believed that the Chinese Communist Party (CCP) bureaucracy was incompetent and corrupt. But the regime didn't tolerate criticism—that is, until 1957. In February of that year, Mao delivered a widely publicized speech in which he said constructive criticism of the party bureaucracy was healthy. It would lead, he said, to a better government.

In what was called the Hundred Flowers Movement, Mao invited people to criticize the government. Millions responded enthusiastically. They wrote letters and published articles detailing the CCP's shortcomings and abuses. They held rallies to demand more intellectual and political freedom. They created posters and paintings that skewered government officials for their stupidity and corruption.

By July 1957 Mao had seen and heard enough. Mao's speech from the previous February—edited to remove any suggestion that he had solicited criticism of the government—was reprinted in the official CCP newspaper as a call to crack down on "rightists" (which basically meant any opponent of China's communist regime). At least 300,000 people who had criticized the government during the Hundred Flowers Movement faced severe retaliation during the "Anti-Rightist Campaign." Some were beaten. Others were sent to "reeducation" camps, where they performed forced labor. Still others were executed. The entire episode served as a stark lesson on the consequences of voicing criticism of Mao or the CCP.

Mao's next major initiative, called the Great Leap Forward, began in early 1958. Mao expected it to rapidly transform China into one of the world's leading economic powers. He also believed that it would solidify support for the CCP.

China's government had already eliminated private ownership of land and forced peasants onto "agricultural producers' cooperatives" consisting of 30 to 50 households each. The Great Leap Forward created huge

Statue of Mao Zedong, who ruled the People's Republic of China from 1949 until his death in 1976.

"people's communes," which on average included about 22,000 people. Mao thought that under the supervision of Communist Party managers, a commune's vast labor pool could be used flexibly and efficiently—not only for the cultivation of crops but also for factory production and the building of big infrastructure projects such as dams, roads, and irrigation systems. In addition, during their every waking hour, commune members would be observed by Communist Party cadres. The cadres would provide constant instruction in communist ideas, and constant reminders of the greatness of Mao. Any sign of discontent or "incorrect" thinking could be dealt with quickly. Chinese peasants' traditional loyalty to family would be replaced with loyalty to Mao and the Communist Party.

For a number of reasons—including Communist Party leaders' ignorance of basic economics and the incompetence and dishonesty of commune

This Soviet propaganda poster from 1931 encourages farmers to accept collectivization and gather the harvest for the good of the Soviet state.

managers—the Great Leap Forward proved disastrous. Crop yields fell, and in 1959 famine broke out across rural China. At first Mao denied that there was any problem. Later he blamed disloyal peasants for hoarding food. But that wasn't true—there was no food to hoard.

Starving peasants fled their communes in search of food. They were forcibly returned—often to be publicly tortured or beaten to death for their disloyalty.

The famine lasted through 1961. In early 1962, China's government finally abandoned the Great Leap Forward and began importing food. The number of people who starved to death during the previous three years will never be known with certainty. Many population experts place the toll at 30 million or more.

In the wake of the catastrophe, Mao's influence waned. Other CCP officials took the lead in policy making. Mao's cult of personality was curtailed, though he was never directly criticized.

Mao wasn't happy with this turn of events. And in 1966, he contrived to regain power by launching the Cultural Revolution. This political movement was supposedly aimed at rooting out "reactionary elements" and "closet capitalists" who, Mao claimed, sought to undermine communism in China. Clearly, however, Mao also meant to target his political rivals in the CCP. Mao unleashed fanatical young followers known as the Red Guard. They assailed intellectuals and other people in positions of authority (including factory managers, teachers, and even parents), people who failed to display sufficient fervor for Mao or the cause of communism, and people suspected of being attached to traditional Chinese culture. Millions of people in these categories were forced to do manual labor, and tens of thousands were executed. Mao once again became China's supreme leader, but at the cost of a decade of social and economic chaos. The Cultural Revolution ended only when Mao died, in 1976.

THE PASSING OF TOTALITARIAN REGIMES

The 20th century's experiments in totalitarian dictatorship brought unspeakable horrors. But for the most part, totalitarian governments didn't

44

last very long. Hitler's Nazi regime was swept away by Allied armies in World War II (as was Mussolini's would-be totalitarian state). Likewise, military force—namely, a 1979 invasion by Vietnam—put an end to the murderous totalitarian regime of Pol Pot and the Khmer Rouge, which ruled Cambodia for just four years.

A military parade in Pyongyang, the capital of North Korea. This country is an example of a modern totalitarian dictatorship. It has been ruled by members of the Kim family for more than 60 years. In 2011 Kim Jong-un succeeded his father, Kim Jong-il, as "supreme leader."

In the Soviet Union and China, totalitarian dictatorships weren't overthrown by force. Rather, these countries evolved away from totalitarianism after the deaths of Stalin and Mao. The successors of Stalin and Mao failed to accrue the same degree of absolute personal power (arguably, they didn't even try to do so). Both countries remained communist states, and they continued to have highly repressive governments. But over time, the regimes became less interested in—and less capable of—controlling all aspects of their citizens' lives. They became, in other words, authoritarian rather than totalitarian regimes.

If totalitarian dictatorships are, as a rule, limited in their longevity, North Korea is a notable exception. For more than six decades, this communist state has remained a totalitarian dictatorship.

A United Nations forensic expert documents evidence from a mass grave in Srebrenica, Bosnia. The victims are among thousands of civilians killed by Bosnian Serb soldiers during the mid-1990s. Dictator Slobodan Milosevic of Yugoslavia encouraged the Serbian attacks on Muslims and Croats. He was later arrested and charged with war crimes and crimes against humanity; however, Milosevic died in prison before his trial was finished.

4

RISE AND FALL OF DICTATORSHIPS

The three decades after World War II saw a dramatic increase in the number of dictatorships across the globe. This wave of authoritarianism can be explained by several factors. One important factor was decolonization. European countries relinquished control of their overseas colonies, mostly in Africa and Asia. After independence, many former colonies failed to develop strong democratic institutions and instead fell into authoritarian rule.

COLD WAR CONSIDERATIONS

Another important factor in the postwar spike in dictatorships was the global struggle between the world's two superpowers, the United States and the Soviet Union. The two countries, which had fought together to defeat Nazi Germany, emerged

During the Cold War (1948–1991), the United States supported "right-wing" dictatorships such as those of Shah Mohammad Reza Pahlavi of Iran (left) and Mobutu Sese Seko of Zaire (bottom), in order to keep countries believed to be strategically important from falling under the rule of communists.

from World War II as rivals. The United States championed liberal democracy, including capitalist economics. The Soviet Union promoted communism. The two systems were incompatible.

Leaders in the Soviet Union believed that the United States intended to eradicate their communist system. Leaders in the United States believed that the Soviet Union sought to spread communism across the world, ultimately stamping out liberal democracy. These mutual suspicions helped create the Cold War, a struggle for dominance between the two superpowers.

Although the United States and the Soviet Union didn't fight each other directly, they did support opposing sides in various "proxy wars." They also sought to enlist allies to their cause from among the world's countries.

The Soviet Union set up communist dictatorships in the countries of Eastern Europe. It also funneled aid to communist dictatorships in North Korea, China (at least until the late 1950s, when Mao broke with the

After being elected president of the Philippines in 1965, Ferdinand E. Marcos gradually seized total control of the government. He closed down the legislature, eliminated freedom of the press, and arrested anyone who opposed his plans for Philippine society. Marcos also transferred billions of dollars in public funds to his personal bank accounts. Despite these actions, the United States backed the Marcos regime for many years because the dictator was a strong opponent of communism. By the mid-1980s, with the Cold War winding down, the United States began to withdraw its support, and a public uprising forced Marcos into exile in 1986.

President Vladimir Putin of Russia and President Hosni Mubarak of Egypt meet in 2006. Mubarak, whose dictatorship was supported by the United States during and after the Cold War, was ousted from power in 2011. Putin came to power through democratic elections in Russia after the collapse of the Soviet Union. Since then he has reversed the movement toward democracy in Russia.

Soviet leadership), and Cuba. Elsewhere the Soviet Union supported leftist insurgencies and leaders with socialist leanings.

Despite its professed democratic ideals, the United States also supported its share of authoritarian regimes during the Cold War. In the eyes of U.S. policymakers, a friendly dictator was preferable to a democratically elected leader with socialist tendencies. In fact, the United States helped overthrow several democratically elected leaders during the Cold War. One was Jacobo Arbenz Guzmán, the president of Guatemala. In 1954 Arbenz was toppled in a U.S.-sponsored coup after he tried to nationalize land held by the U.S.-based United Fruit Company. A 36-year-long civil war ensued.

Another democratically elected leader ousted in a U.S.-supported coup was Chile's Salvador Allende. An avowed communist, Allende died during the 1973 coup that brought to power a military junta headed by General Augusto Pinochet. Pinochet would gain a reputation for brutality. Opponents of his regime were routinely tortured and, in many cases, murdered.

By the late 1980s, the Cold War had begun to wind down. It was over definitively by 1991, when the Soviet Union collapsed. For many dictators around the world, the end of the Cold War spelled the end of external support for their regimes. Many dictatorships that had been maintained or aided by the United States or the Soviet Union fell. Often they were replaced by democratic governments. This process was especially noticeable in Eastern Europe and Latin America. Still, dictatorships remained across much of Africa and parts of Asia.

THE DICTATOR'S SUPPORT

No dictatorship can survive without some domestic support. At minimum, a dictator must have the loyalty of armed forces, police, or paramilitary organizations—groups that could use violence to remove the dictator from power (and that the dictator can enlist, if necessary, to violently suppress opposition).

Most dictators, however, have additional sources of support.

Omar al-Bashir, president of the Republic of the Sudan, is among the world's most infamous and controversial dictators today. He has been charged by the International Criminal Court with committing "crimes against humanity" for ordering mass murders in southern Sudan and the Darfur region of western Sudan. However, Bashir is unlikely to face trial for his actions so long as he remains in power in Sudan.

Lee Hsien-Loong, the son of Singapore's longtime authoritarian leader Lee Kuan Yew, became the country's prime minister in 2004. Since Yew's retirement from Singaporean politics in 2011, Lee Hsien-Loong has been the most powerful politician in the country.

Typically, dictators deliver concrete benefits to certain groups. Often these benefits are economic. In some cases dictators directly provide employment or money to their supporters. In other cases they merely maintain an economic system that allows specific groups to profit.

Some dictators draw support from a particular national, ethnic, or religious group, which they may play off against other groups. Robert Mugabe, for example, relies on members of his own Shona tribe for his base of support. Slobodan Milosevic, the former dictator of Yugoslavia, appealed constantly to Serb nationalism while disparaging Croats and Muslims. The regime of Iraq's Saddam Hussein, which was dominated by members of the country's Sunni Arab minority, oppressed Iraqi Kurds and Shia Muslims.

The broader a dictatorship's base of support, the more stable that dictatorship is likely to be. Still, all dictators confront the problem of legitimacy in a way that democratic systems do not.

THE PROBLEM OF SUCCESSION

Another problem faced by dictatorships is succession. Democratic systems have accepted rules for the transfer of power from one leader to another. Dictatorships do not.

Many dictators are removed only by force or upon the dictator's natural death. And when a dictator dies, a violent struggle for power often results.

Some dictatorships have attempted to resolve the problem of succession in the manner of hereditary monarchies: by passing power from father to son. After the death of François "Papa Doc" Duvalier in 1971, his son, Jean-Claude "Baby Doc"

> To secure their power, dictators often quash the voices of their nation's most educated citizens. Teachers, scientists, and businesspeople may be forced out of the country or killed. This "brain drain" often makes it extremely difficult for countries to recover even after the dictator is no longer in power.

Duvalier became dictator of Haiti. A popular uprising forced Baby Doc from power in 1986. Syria's Bashar al-Assad succeeded his father, Hafez al-Assad, in 2000. In North Korea, dictatorial power has passed from father to son not once, but twice: from Kim Il-sung to Kim Jong-il in 1994, and from Kim Jong-il to Kim Jong-un in 2011.

Fidel Castro, the longtime dictator of Cuba, found a different way to keep power in the family when he became too ill to govern. In 2008 he passed the reins to his younger brother, Raúl Castro.

THE FUTURE OF DICTATORSHIP

In rare instances, an authoritarian ruler governs without corrupt motives, and in a manner that clearly benefits the majority of his country's citizens. This sort of authoritarian ruler is sometimes called a "benevolent dictator." Lee Kuan Yew is a case in point.

Lee's island country, Singapore, was a British possession until after World War II. In 1959 Singapore became self-governing. The new government was set up as a democracy, but within a few years Lee's People's Action Party (PAP) had assumed complete control. Under Lee and the PAP, labor unions were severely restricted, the government controlled the media, people could be imprisoned without trial, and election guidelines were crafted to ensure the PAP's continued control. "I make no apologies that the PAP is the government and the government is the PAP," Lee said bluntly in 1984, after a quarter century in power. Despite his antidemocratic practices, Lee was quite popular with Singapore's citizens because his policies led to a booming economy and a better standard of living for most people on the island.

Benevolent dictators like Lee are, however, very much the exception. And, in the 21st century, democratic governance has become the expectation of people across the globe.

Still, authoritarian governments persist, as the Freedom in the World survey attests. Produced by the Washington, D.C.-based nongovernmental organization Freedom House, the annual survey evaluates political rights and civil rights in all of the world's countries. The 2011 Freedom in

The deposed president of Iraq, Saddam Hussein, sits before an Iraqi judge at the start of his trial in 2004. The dictator ruled Iraq from the late 1970s until the spring of 2003, when an invasion led by the U.S. military drove him from power. Saddam was captured and placed on trial for the murder of hundreds of Iraqis carried out by his regime. He was found guilty and executed in 2006.

the World survey judged nearly half of the world's countries (48 percent) as not free. Almost all of these authoritarian regimes were in Africa, Asia, and the Middle East.

Change appeared to be coming to the Middle East, however. Democracy protests swept through the region—beginning in Tunisia in late 2010—in what would be dubbed the Arab Spring. Longtime dictatorships were toppled in Tunisia, Egypt, and Libya, and by the summer of 2012 the Syrian regime also appeared to be teetering. The Arab Spring provided further evidence that the pull of freedom is indeed powerful.

CHAPTER NOTES

p. 9:   "If yesterday I fought . . ." Anthony Lewis, "Abroad at Home; The Corruption of Power," *New York Times*, April 22, 2000. http://www.nytimes.com/2000/04/22/opinion/abroad-at-home-the-corruption-of-power.html

p. 10: "You have the jewel . . ." Doris Lessing, "The Jewel of Africa," *New York Review of Books*, April 10, 2003.

p. 15: "They killed hundreds . . ." *Fresh Air*, "A Journalist Bears Witness to Mugabe's Massacre." NPR, March 30, 2011. http://www.npr.org/2011/03/30/134955995/a-journalist-bears-witness-to-mugabes-massacre

p. 17: "Power tends to corrupt . . ." Roland Hill, *Lord Acton* (New Haven, CT: Yale University Press, 1993), 300.

p. 32: "The Fascist conception . . ." Benito Mussolini and Giovanni Gentile, "The Doctrine of Fascism" (1932). http://www.worldfuturefund.org/wffmaster/reading/germany/mussolini.htm

p. 33:   "I believe in the genius . . ." Tracy H. Koon, *Believe, Obey, Fight: Political Socialization of Youth in Fascist Italy, 1922–1943* (Chapel Hill: University of North Carolina Press, 1985), 154.

p. 36: "With pride we see . . ." David Jablonsky, *Churchill and Hitler: Essays on the Political-Military Direction of Total War* (Ilford, Essex, England: Frank Cass & Co., 1994), 22.

p. 54: "I make no apologies . . ." Terence Chong (ed.), *Management of Success: Singapore Revisited* (Singapore: Institute of Southeast Asian Studies, 2010), 72.

CHRONOLOGY

44 BCE: Julius Caesar declares himself Rome's "Dictator for Life."

1800s: Caudillos come to power in Latin American states that have gained independence from Spain.

1922: The Soviet Union is officially founded. Benito Mussolini takes power in Italy.

1928: Joseph Stalin becomes undisputed leader of the Soviet Union, begins establishing a totalitarian dictatorship.

1933: After being named chancellor of Germany, Adolf Hitler takes dictatorial power.

1939–45: World War II.

1948: Kim Il-sung establishes communist dictatorship in North Korea.

1949: Mao Zedong proclaims the founding of the communist People's Republic of China.

1953: Stalin dies.

1959–61: China's Great Famine.

1973: Chilean president Salvador Allende is overthrown in a U.S.-supported military coup that brings General Augusto Pinochet to power.

1976: Mao dies.

1980: Robert Mugabe elected prime minister of newly independent Zimbabwe.

1991: The Soviet Union collapses, bringing an end to the Cold War.

2010: The "Arab Spring" begins with protests in Tunisia.

2011: Kim Jong-un succeeds his father, Kim Jong-il, as "supreme leader" of North Korea.

2012: A movement to overthrow dictator Bashar al-Assad leads to civil war in Syria.

GLOSSARY

ANTI-SEMITISM—hostility toward or hatred of Jews.

AUTHORITARIANISM—a governing system or philosophy that demands the obedience of citizens; dictatorship.

CADRES—trained and highly motivated members of a revolutionary party.

CAPITALISM—an economic system that permits the ownership of private property, allows individuals and companies to compete for their own economic gain, and generally lets free market forces determine the price of goods and services.

COMMUNISM—a political and economic system that champions the elimination of private property and common ownership of goods, for the benefit of all members of society.

COUP—the sudden, often violent overthrow of a government by an individual or a small group.

GENOCIDE—the deliberate and systematic destruction of a racial or cultural group.

IDEOLOGY—a systematic set of principles and goals.

INDOCTRINATE—to teach or instruct in a biased way.

JUNTA—a government led by a group of military leaders.

NATIONALISM—promotion of the interests of one's own nation above the interests of other nations.

PARAMILITARY—relating to a force organized along military lines but not composed of official soldiers.

PROPAGANDA—communication that seeks to promote a certain viewpoint, often by using biased information.

TOTALITARIANISM—an extreme form of authoritarianism in which the state seeks to control all aspects of citizens' lives.

FURTHER READING

FOR STUDENTS:

Arnold, James R., and Roberta Wiener. *Robert Mugabe's Zimbabwe*. Minneapolis: Twenty-First Century Books, 2008.

Behnke, Alison. *Kim Jong Il's North Korea*. Minneapolis, MN: Twenty-First Century Books, 2008.

Cunningham, Kevin. *Joseph Stalin and the Soviet Union*. Greensboro, NC: Morgan Reynolds Publishing, 2006.

Fandel, Jennifer. *Dictatorship*. Mankato, MN: Creative Education, 2008.

Haugen, Brenda. *Adolf Hitler: Dictator of Nazi Germany*. Minneapolis, MN: Compass Point Books, 2006.

FOR ADULTS:

Ezrow, Natasha M. *Dictators and Dictatorships: Understanding Authoritarian Regimes and Their Leaders*. New York: Continuum, 2011.

Gandhi, Jennifer. *Political Institutions Under Dictatorship*. New York: Cambridge University Press, 2008.

Godwin, Peter. *The Fear: Robert Mugabe and the Martyrdom of Zimbabwe*. New York: Little, Brown and Company, 2011.

Snyder, Timothy. *Bloodlands: Europe Between Hitler and Stalin*. New York: Basic Books, 2010.

Wintrobe, Ronald. *The Political Economy of Dictatorship*. New York: Cambridge University Press, 1998.

INTERNET RESOURCES

http://www.gresham.ac.uk/search/node/dictatorship

This site links to several pages examining the "age of dictatorship" in Europe and the Soviet Union during the early part of the 20th century.

http://www.africandictator.org/

This site discusses the rule of dictators throughout the African continent.

http://www.cnn.com/SPECIALS/1999/china.50/inside.china/profiles/mao.tsetung/

This page offers a biography of Mao Zedong.

http://www.livius.org/di-dn/dictator/dictator.html

This site examines the governmental institution of dictatorship in ancient Rome, covering various individuals and examining their powers.

INDEX

CONTRIBUTORS

Senior Consulting Editor **TIMOTHY J. COLTON** is Morris and Anna Feldberg Professor of Government and Russian Studies and is the chair of the Department of Government at Harvard University. His books include *The Dilemma of Reform in the Soviet Union* (1986); *Moscow: Governing the Socialist Metropolis* (1995), which was named best scholarly book in government and political science by the Association of American Publishers; *Transitional Citizens: Voters and What Influences Them in the New Russia* (2000); and *Popular Choice and Managed Democracy: The Russian Elections of 1999 and 2000* (with Michael McFaul, 2003). Dr. Colton is a member of the editorial board of World Politics and Post-Soviet Affairs.

DIANE BAILEY has written more than twenty nonfiction books for children and teens, on topics ranging from sports to states. She also writes fiction, and looks forward to the release of her first murder mystery novel in 2012. As a freelance editor, Diane works to help authors who write fiction for children and young adults. Diane lives in Kansas with her two sons and two dogs.